Children of Ararat addresses the legacy of the Armenian genocide. A son shaped by his father's experience serves as witness to the aftershocks of brutality. This poet is unafraid to face the horror that is too often the result of politics and too much the truth of history.

~ *Jury, Dektet 2010*

ALSO BY KEITH GAREBIAN:

Hugh Hood
Hugh Hood and his Works
William Hutt: a Theatre Portrait
Leon Rooke and his Works
A Well-Bred Muse: Selected Theatre Writings 1978-1988
George Bernard Shaw and Christopher Newton:
   Explorations of Shavian Theatre
The Making of 'My Fair Lady'
The Making of 'Gypsy'
The Making of 'West Side Story'
William Hutt: Masks and Faces
The Making of 'Cabaret'
Pain: Journeys Around My Parents
The Making of 'Guys and Dolls'
Reservoir of Ancestors
Frida: Paint Me as a Volcano
Blue: The Derek Jarman Poems

children
of ararat

KEITH GAREBIAN

Frontenac House
Calgary, Alberta

Book and cover design: Epix Design
Cover Image: Armenian orphans at the Gyumri Orphanage gates;
photograph by Armin T. Wedner, 1915; collection of Near East Relief Society.
Author photo: David Young

Library and Archives Canada Cataloguing in Publication

Garebian, Keith, 1943-
    Children of Ararat / Keith Garebian.

Poems.
ISBN 978-1-897181-32-4

    I. Title.

PS8563.A645C55 2010   C811'.6   C2009-907338-2

We acknowledge the support of the Canada Council for the Arts for our
publishing program and the support of the Alberta Creative Development
Initiative. We also acknowledge the support of The Alberta Foundation for
the Arts.

Canada Council   Conseil des Arts
for the Arts   du Canada

Alberta Foundation for the Arts

Printed and bound in Canada
Published by Frontenac House Ltd.
1138 Frontenac Avenue S.W.
Calgary, Alberta, T2T 1B6, Canada
Tel: 403-245-2491 Fax: 403-245-2380
editor@frontenachouse.com   www.frontenachouse.com

In Memoriam: Adam Garebian
(1909-1995)

ACKNOWLEDGEMENTS

Some poems in this book appeared previously in a different version (and sometimes with a different title) in the following: my memoir, *Pain: Journeys Around My Parents* (2000); my first poetry book, *Reservoir of Ancestors* (2003); the Armenian Poetry Project blog (created and edited by Lola Koundakjian); and *Exile*. "Dikranagerd", in a slightly different form, won First Prize in the Canadian Authors Association (Niagara Branch) Poetry Contest and was published in *The Saving Bannister, Vol. 24,* along with "July in Diyarbekir". "Elegy for William Saroyan" was selected Poem of the Month (November 2009) by the Parliamentary Poet-Laureate.

Thanks to the Ontario Arts Council for a Writers' Reserve Grant (as recommended by Tsar Publications) and a Works In Progress Grant that helped me complete the book. Thanks to Linda Pastan: her poem "Grudnow" inspired my poem "Dikranagerd". Thanks to Allan Briesmaster and Don Mills for their positive comments on the preliminary draft; to Atom Egoyan for permission to use quotations from his film *Calendar*; to Barry Callaghan for selecting seven of the poems for *Exile*; to Henry Beissel, Joy Kogawa, and Peter Balakian for their warm, enthusiastic encouragement; to George Elliott Clarke, bill bissett, and Alice Major for selecting this manuscript for the Dektet 2010 series; and, most particularly, to Mick Burrs, a poet and editor of exemplary taste, sophisticated critical perception, painstaking care, and warm empathy, who edited and helped me fine-tune the manuscript so that craft would never be relinquished to mere passion.

CONTENTS

PART ONE: ADAM

❁

landfall speaks a blessing
the other side of dying
helps you navigate the seasons

now, your face full of hours
your hair early gray
heavy on scales of grief

speak my name
pull me to you
your hand grappling my heart

DISCOVERY

They were there for most of a century,
eyes fallen out,
teeth missing,
set in clay
wall of a hill in northern Syria,
where water cannot sink
lower than clay
next to the Harbur River,
water with black secrets.

The more he digs with his car keys
the more skulls slide,
collapsing into paste
as the wet air touches
calcium for the first time
since a thousand bodies
disappeared.

The lost tribe
overtaken and now silent
for the rest of time
like the terracotta army
of a Chinese emperor.

But these are no soldiers
in the hillside by the river,
trapped by sects
of fanatical belief.
They are white scars,
remnants of a human image
deeply hidden
outcries buried
in suppliant gestures
underground massacres
and the stink of race.

Bone becomes paste
around him,
ivory turns dull.

Backbones, femurs, joints,
and a black cord
eternally bound
to what are sunk
away from the upper world.

Eye sockets
staring at him
as the sky looks cold blue.
Black holes
where sight should be
covered with clay
that lies most of a century
over their faces.

His fingers probe
for amulets, rings,
shreds of cloth,
some handwriting
of their lives
and intimate selves.
Clay is the book
of these dead
who lie with broken stones
profaned yet innocent
in a still hillside.

He stands and draws
a deep breath
swallows all
he can of desecration.

CEREMONY TO PROTECT MOTHER AND CHILD

Seek a midwife who can fold the evening into her long skirt.
Give her a long metal skewer – not for torture, but for liberation.
Let her blacken its point in the *tonir's* fire. Molten metal for
    alchemy.
Let her draw the sign of the cross on each wall to keep the devil
    away.
Let her hand the skewer to the labouring mother with a prayer.
Let her make a path from the door for an angel.
Let her give the visiting angel a bag to gather the mother's sins.
Let the angel hold the bag over the mother's head when the child
    is born, and sprinkle the sins back on the mother.
Let the midwife cut the umbilical cord and smear blood over the
    child's waxy face to make healthy red cheeks.
Let the midwife wrap the after-birth and cord in a white cloth
    for burial in the churchyard so the child will grow into a fine
    chorister.
Let the midwife beat salt and eggs into warm water for the
    child's first bath.
Let the midwife anoint the child's head, arms, and feet with salt,
    then swaddle him in warm clothes.
Let her keep the child swaddled for forty days.
Let the neighbours' children rush out with sweets for the village.

NB: Ceremonies are not celestial absolutes.
When enacting the sixth rule, beware:
If the door is open just a crack, you may see too much to be
    really safe.
And the angel says nothing in patient holiness.

MY FATHER

1. To Speak His Own Love

Named Adam, he wasn't the first-born,
yet he felt a wound in his side,
something wrenched from him
in Eden, and he was cast out
among weeds and bare stones
never to be free of wariness,
even when held by desire,
making it hard to speak his own love
from a fixed place in the world.

2. Silence and Stammer

Ash on his orphaned tongue
weight of the void

he stammered into stone, into silence
the nothingness of night

    words speaking stones
    stones speaking silence

dry tongue feeling around
the seams of syllables

stammer in the dryness of exile
spells the distance unforgiving

his murdered kin, the shadows looming
dark birds hammering the sky

AN ODYSSEUS

My father an Odysseus
lost since his city fell,
wandered with devices
on his side of the wall
between us, a wall built
by himself, by an army
of shadows hidden in crannies
far from olive trees and cypresses,
little lamps on stony hills
pocked with silence.

The desert his sea,
his eyes watering with glare,
his father in a dust-cloud's mouth,
his mother in a ravine,
the sands heaving beneath the crew
of starving orphans.

His mind tossed on the sea
so wide, it took years to cross,
its spray spitting on his face, his pain.

THE PLUM TREE

The plum tree, its fruit bent low with sweetness.
Your mother's life bent and broken.

Lake Van so blue with sadness.
Your mother's lips mourning blue.

Butchers and tanners with clubs and cleavers.
Your mother screaming as an axe smashed doors.

The moon gliding softly in a silver loop.
Your mother's heart ripped in a blackened country.

The plum tree stands where it always stood.
And your mother's blood feeding its roots.

FLOTSAM

A cemetery where your mother disappeared before
you could return with water to soothe her blistered lips.

Rich with bodies, the dry turf yielded
no secret of her vanishing.
She was lost in your sobbing, noon
prickling your boyish mind.

Later you would learn she was lifted into a cart,
dumped into a ravine, her face dissolving
in the crimson river's current, her body
a floating shadow amid cruising fish.

She had gone with the waters like flotsam.
And you wondered if she would
wind up somewhere clean, entwining
herself with flowers in the earth's seasonal love.

JULY IN DIYARBEKIR

Cloudless blue and no wind to ruffle
partridge in olive trees
or even a silk scarf.

Islands of mulberries,
watermelon pregnant with pink juice,
the Tigris changing colour on a whim,
flat tile roofs covered with white cloth
to keep sleep cool.

The people loved these wonders with constancy
of custom, not knowing
July would be a killing month,
human nature turned into a bestiary.

If they had put their ears to the ground,
they would have heard blood gushing
in Aintab, Harput, Sivas, Yozgut.

And their kinfolk at the mercy of a new science,
vivisection and its fresh possibilities.
Flesh opened as if for a butcher carving into sheep,
the remains turned into scraps
for vultures, whose long necks unscrolled
in ravenous swoops.

In the clean evening light
the city hulled baskets of bulghur,
sticking to work as shopkeepers disappeared,
children taken from their school.
Women at the baths went clean to grief.

Work kept others from thinking
about the unbelievable.

July became a month of tendons
and sinews, the fitful vulnerability
of flesh, death by wholesale subtraction.

Between the staked olive trees, the partridge
caught their spurs in wires,
wrenching the sky with cries.

HIS ROARING

You are long gone underground
and you've cheated the maggots
giving yourself to fire
so they have nothing but ash.

But your voice has not gone.
I carry it in my head
as I write this poem
about a dead man
whose every second thought was of death.

You were the prophet
of the mad language of man
no other animal understands.

You could never whisper, only shout
above the factory din,
bedlam of machines
crying to get free of their skins.

You shouted your love
sharp as a mosquito sting
high above the jasmine
as I tried to quell
the ear-numbing thunder
of your adamantine will.

And when you spoke of your past –
the whole mad history of it:
mother, father,
sisters, cousins, aunts
stalked and gouged
by the huge black bird of death,
and heard in their wails
the brotherhood of prey,
there was no gentle message,

no bleating lamb of God
but a shaking, quaking vision

and a roaring which carries me
to the end of this world.

THIRST

My father, on the ravaged side
of my family, drank
when he was brooding. He drank
whiskey and soda, gin, beer,
and something called *hootch*,
fermented in rubber bladders
in sand or dry mud, made
of mashed skins, rotten pulpy fruit,
and God knows what else,
soaked in resentment against Prohibition
and Indian taxes on foreign booze.

In his cacophonous factory,
smelling of new plastic and oil,
workers thickened the air with curses,
machinery clanged, sparks flew,
the din of labour soaked
him in sweat. So he drank
to dim the bodies in stress,
drown the noise, and he drank
to temper the heat of work,
his thirst leading him beyond the gates
where clang and clatter settled in his bones.

Yet, he didn't die of drink but
another thirst.
What swam in his blood
was more than alcohol – a debt
he felt unable to pay to ancestors
trapped in a desert's stench of death,
shrivelled skins fermenting in a vat
of bubbling heat.

Blackening flesh, terrible
ragged cries, skeleton arms
uplifted to silent skies
made his thirst bitter,
made him drunk and roar
for remembered wreckage.

And the useless pity of friends
outside the darkness of his blood
surged, surged as he drank, knowing

that nothing
would make his life
holy and right again.

DROWNED MOONS

Their faces the shapes of water
flowing amorphous
under cliffs black with clay.

Their eyes, drowned moons,
mouths fluted with silence,
ghosts in marrow,
turning in currents.

An April of dissolving melancholy
steeped in blue.
Easter is wet with sacrifice,
bodies too profuse to save.

Nothing bright is risen.
What lifts is
dumb, uncovered.

THE BLINDNESS OF INFECTED WATER

Were you pretending to see as children do
who do not know how they come by such sight –
a mystery without language
because there were only things
to take for granted, as your eyes
closed and the world passed
in a flicker and nothing was worse
or better? Eyes were innocent
before the mouth found words for the heart.

You thirsted, but the sea was invisibly far,
and your thirst was a daily errand.
The sun was cruel, no shade
between dawn and midday,
midday and midnight.

They gave you infected water to wash your dirt,
and it bathed you in blindness – and guilt.

You suddenly went blind, you thought,
because your fathers changed their faith.
You thought you turned blind
because God saw this betrayal
and drew a veil across your eyes.
You thought God struck you blind from shame
for what you might have known
of his cruel glare that banished you from hope.

But your eyes in their blindness
cannot see worms and scorpions,
cannot see bodies burned the colour of gangrene,
cannot see the dance of devils on your parents' graves.

DIKRANAGERD

When he talked of Dikranagerd
my father's eyes vanished
into a town sometimes Turkish,
sometimes Russian,
history as swift as a flood,
roots swept away
with crops and trees, fields
dissolving, everything muddied.

The only permanence – Ararat,
its white caps neither growing
nor breaking, awaiting
some angel to deliver
the landscape:
the stone-faced churches,
rocky fields,
oxen pressed each to each for heat
like dark orphans in pictures.

Perhaps I would have died with history,
grandparents and aunts, a whole tribe
uprooted from metallic ground,
hard as the heels of assassins,
or the bones left by ravenous dogs
too weak to chew them.

My father always sipped his tea noisily,
teeth braced the way he flinched
from memories, no sugar cube
to sweeten his loss,
slowly re-tasting his life
in slurps, a far-away look in his eyes
once gold in Dikranagerd.

NOMAD: ADDRESSED TO MY FATHER
AND MYSELF

Day and night know where you move, carrying the desert
with/in you. The repetitive desert you are never wholly
done with. The most cruel sun teaches perplexity of loss in
all the days to come after the whirring of scythes, the flayed
tongue's rasp. Sand snowing on your silence, you walk
between rage and memory, feet crimsoning the earth,
tracks leading back to childhood, mother hanging linen on a line,
father moving amid the bleat of goats to the family factory,
the smell and hiss of iron furnaces, the air
breathing promise and calmness, suckling you with the
strength of inheritance.

All lost. You will never know yourself again, wandering
with fever in your lungs,
heart hollowed. You cannot know why your kin
have breathed themselves to nothing, or why you have no words
large enough to hold them.

Now the sky pins a doomed star on your breast, the clouds
as witness. Disaster haunts
you to the brink of desolation. No brethren in light or
dark –

you become a nomad, violent heir
to a blighted harvest
in merciless acres.

BLOOD MEMORY

In a mid-Eastern town (still not known to me), when he was in
his very early twenties, my father almost killed a young Muslim
who had insulted Christians. Not that he was religious. Could
it have been revenge against memory? At his work site (also
unknown to me), he almost drowned the victim in a tank of
water, blood memory rushing to his brain. He couldn't erase the
bodies of the slaughtered caught in a hypnotic plea. When he
inhaled, he smelled something dying and something newly born.

The scene of near-murder printed on his mind was much smaller
than the one of desert sky, dunes looming like mocking monsters,
and the staggering caravan, mouths of silent O's. At night, the
moon overflowed with blood.

The Koran could not protect his victim against my father's brief
ecstasy. When my father seized the man by the neck and shook
him the way a maddened dog shakes a rat, he said nothing,
but inside him a silent cry came from a place of tragedy, the
place where he was trapped as a boy between the living and
the dead. Something in him had withered away from that time,
but something else had grown. A plague of anger out of his
lucid nightmares about the past. His rage made him special,
separating him from those who do not rage.

He almost killed, in consideration of his murdered kin. But he
did not, because his fellow-workers pulled him off the choking
victim, who was of a tribe in fear of their own fear. A fear of
discovering that guilt deepens the longer it waits for expiation.

Other things deepen, too.
Under the old heart of despair
grows another heart that fears to hope.

I HAVE INHERITED YOU

I have inherited you,
your voice in my head
a pressure, a haunting
that will outlast me,
unless I heed it, record
a moving storm
across the electric sky.

A history is never simple,
nor the legacy of a world completely
changed. Time forgets us all,
glitter of lives, taste of dreams,
once bodies are moulded
to earth, sunk into sea, sent
shuddering into air
blowing away purpose.

ITEMS RETRIEVED FROM MY FATHER'S ROOM

Clock radio with a rundown battery,
gauze pads, Q-Tips for his waxy ears.

Cigarette lighter, table-cloth with nicotine stains,
Thick crystal ashtray, shadowed with residue.

Harness for his damaged neck,
my dead sister's last needlework.

Small bowl with buttons, a threader,
bread crumbs on the kitchen table.

Mismatched socks, a walking stick,
toe-nail clippers, body lotion.

Armenian pamphlets, *The Last Days of Musa Dagh*,
tall lamp in hand-carved walnut, his retirement gift.

Magnifying glass, medical prescriptions,
a list of grievances in block letters.

PART TWO: REVELATIONS

❋

SQUALID

Everything is begging to be given voice:
empty work-sheds, rusted keyholes, deserted cafés,
the vines of orchards, blue shadows,
shrivelled shoes, abandoned flutes –

If only just to say:
To have died here
    had some meaning
        in the squalid mess of history –

        So we may forgive the insult
        of this, the cheering of mobs
        as axes thudded, as bright blood
        filled the gutters –

        And fires left their scars
        down to the last ungrieving stone.

DEKTETS IN HOMAGE

1.

The clouds are electric around Ararat.
Some of the dead burn fissures in the sky.

When I look at the mountain, I see Noah's ark
empty and forlorn, broken by the flood.

It could not help the unicorn,
the one who fled and drowned.

Was God envious of my father's people?
Did God force them to die together?

The stars of the universe are not all diamonds.
Some burn as they fall.

2.

Sun and moon have their way with the orphans of Ararat,
unintended companions in mass murder.

The caravan of urchins staggers through sand,
dust and stones photographing their faces.

For me, the past plays over and over.
Dust collects in dunes. Scars are plagues.

Do you think I am talking only of my father's orphaned life?
It is I who am now trapped in an abyss.

I tell you the truth about this deserted horde of orphans
so their eternity may touch my lips.

3.

The orphaned survivors are alive with instinct.
They play in shadows, bewildered.

Their fathers ploughed fields and fertilized their minds
while their enemies sharpened their daggers, caressed their clubs.

At night they remember their mothers' gentle breath.
This is when love cries out with special yearning.

What spirit is found in places of slaughter?
A new Adam learning to begin again.

Is re-creating a nightmare blasphemy?
The brutality of facts cannot go into darkness silently.

4.

"What is the fault of children?" a grandmother asks,
her lament resounding from Harput to Syria.

A bullet responds.
Her voice vanishes as a thin mist.

The children are forced into widening circles on naked feet,
the hot sand bringing them no closer to home.

The hours fall like dead flies.
The shuddering sky unnerves the urchins.

In the solitude of sleep, horrors multiply.
With torn swelling feet, only a few will remember everything.

5.

These words supplement what my father remembered.
These words are a supplement to myself.

Dreams are a strange language created on Ararat,
far above the poppies, blown into sleep.

The violence of sore feet and dry throats is repeated.
The repentance for surviving this violence.

Scavenger dogs sink sharp teeth into the dying,
their impartiality serving the cruelty of men.

Sometimes we feel guilty for deserting our hate.
Should we leave the dead, care only for the living?

FIBONACCI POEMS AND VARIATIONS

Ritual

Should
we
torture
rape and kill
then pray to Allah
the All-Merciful for reward?

Collection

Did
they
desire
boys for work
or carnal pleasure –
Hamid's Ottoman officers?

Civilization

Was
it
Europe
cleaning knives
with elegant cloth
for the mad Sultan and his killers?

Soup

Grass,
weeds,
buds, leaves
make a soup
in a battered copper pot –
they drink and they vomit, these starving Armenians.

Medicine

A
love
for facts
and unvarnished truth
proves too strong a dose
for diehard deniers who cough up daily falsehoods.

Question

Who
chose
this history
we have lived
for centuries in ruined Eden
enduring holocausts by murderers who cancel all truth?

Arrival

We
leave
a place
of sudden knives
slicing into young and old
to arrive where death burns through our skin.

EATING SHOES: THE JOURNEY

1.

They ate mouldy shoes boiled for three days.
Their hands which had grown vegetables, surrounded
by cows and dogs, lifted limp laces like pasta.

The roots of their hunger remembered
kitchens and *tonirs* baking *lavash*,
assiduous aunts toiling near ovens,
fierce chain-smoking uncles, tussling children,
pimply adolescents blushing among fat flowers,
green vine leaves climbing webbings,
the glitter of finned fish,
spicy oils and raw meats slashed
for grilling. In the orchards,
black grapes grew dark with dreams
and pomegranates ripe with ruby fire.

2.

But they were marching somewhere
in the desert's furnace, seeking caves
where they could scoop out refuge
before blood became a processional
underground. They wanted shoes to plod
blistering stones, their skeletal bodies
ragged in despair, bony heads on stick frames.

A lucky few found corpses with shoes,
knelt in the black furrows of death,
and plucked up paltry leather
to make meals from plunder.

3.

Dull jawed, they ate hide
as if it were prime beef,
forced it down their raw throats,
mouths creating juice, minds
pushing back death with bony fingers.

Boiled shoes would give them life
so their naked feet might move
through calendars of bayonets,
burning winds ringing in their ears,
eyes cooked by a saturnine sun.

Shoes had passed from feet to feet,
age to age, rubbed and scuffed by stones,
joints glued like perfect sockets,
relics of animals on dry steppes.
Heels broke apart like bones,
tongues of hide tore in flaps,
all chewed, dark strings
and straps, after the cauldron.

They ate as slow steam came
over soles, and pieces were gnashed
to nothing, and when they were full,
small nails were left for ravenous dogs.

4.

Leather fed bad dreams,
delirium, ghosts.
Centuries of Ottoman heels
on necks the colour of sand.

The desert ached
and days were warped with grief.

Time stumbled over the shoes, fell
through holes into the seams of rocks
where names disappeared
in the dank smell of clay.

5.

Scimitars sliced the horizon.

TWO PHOTOGRAPHS

1. Cut

Dressed in fezzes and uniforms,
moustaches thicker than their lips,

sinewy arms crossed in proud distinction,
they sit as *pashas* at a table,

staring straight at the camera lens
while two heads
lie on platters
spattered with blood.

One moment defining what they did
in their spare time before dreaming up

reasons to round off
genocide to zero.

2. This Is a Tool

This is a tool for chopping cotton
now used for Armenian flesh.

A strong leg gouged pitilessly,
a firm tendon slashed with impunity.

Blood doesn't retreat from a sharp edge
but is reduced as the lips go blue.

The flesh is real and so is the leg
and they belong to a man

who screams
like the boy brained in another room.

TATTOOED GIRLS, PART ONE

See where the dots and small X's
blue the skin. Eyes go empty
like shells, where light reclines
on young faces before shrinking
into the dark again. No almond
oil can relieve the burn
of insignia on cheeks and foreheads,
necks and chins. No turban,
no shawl, no locket conceal
the enforced bond of young flesh
and perverse misogynist whim.

The waters of childhood have gone
from Melek and Victoria, Anig
and Khatoun. One with thin arms crossed
at her bosom, one with a locket
like a kiss at her neck, another scarved
like a sultan's fresh whore.
Palms red from henna juice,
their brandings an extravagance
counted in coins.

As time beats down memories of home,
they crouch and bend a little more,
watch the flames hiss up to their darkened cheeks,
stir the pot thicker in the crackling heat.

Olive oil, goat meat, cheese and figs,
small voices chattering over flame pits,
they are chained to a fate
memorialized, obscene.

TATTOOED GIRLS, PART TWO

1.

Breathing odours foreign to them,
they are seized with intent
to blow old idioms shut.
A catalogue of harms in the insistent
abduction, playing the slave
with irresistible wounds.

New enchantment means harsh entry
that rends old families, taking a path
after the loss of graves, walking to the salt
and bread of a different closure –
time bringing the future
into an enclosed presence.
In heart song's harsh music,
ecstasy is absent from gestures
in submission's bond.

2.

Woman has become a doubt
despite the prospect of fecundity
and inheritance. Their tattoos have meaning
only as functions of the body: to labour,
cook, clean, bear children, submit
to what is outside their skin, keeping within
a clamp on private configuration,
the blue wounds altering the visage,
linking arm, chest, neck, and face.
Even with food, their roots find soil bitter,
the historical rupture forbidding rapture.

Tattoos are drawn on them
like scars or yearnings.

Skin is hazard's shroud.
Its markings hone a homily
of enactment, the body's capacity
to turn frailty to fortuitous torsion,
endowment, dissimulation.
Without panic, they survive
the twist of surfaces, gathering
solitude and pain under the ribs,
straining to remember small realities
and cherished faces.

Memorizing water in their mouths
where rain had entered, the wind
a caress in their hair, and home
a place where feelings erupted
no matter what they willed.

Skin trammelled from the outside
can rise with the mind's fabulation,
the will's inexact fervour, the spine's
shudder, leaning with the secret self
to a stillness beyond amazement –

a course of sustenance in a wounded domain,
the heart's small crater.

THIRTEEN WAYS OF LOOKING AT 1915

1.

Between Great and Little Ararat,
their broad-shouldered domes,
looms the cry of the Ottoman Turk.

2.

I am of two minds about 1915.
Like Ararat
where the great chasm runs
far into its own heart.

3.

If we cannot define 1915
it is because we don't know it well.
I wheel around two propositions:
Ataturk's "He's a lucky man who can say,
'I am a Turk.'"
And his lapidary phrase:
"We resemble ourselves."

4.

1915 was a slaughterer's year
pouring out death in innumerable buckets.

5.

I do not know which to prefer –
the proud declamation:
"We are a nation of many enemies."
Or the coded innuendo:
"Take care of the Armenians."
I do not know which to prefer –
the Ottoman's concept of honour,
or his notion of kinship.

6.

1915. Before. During. After.
In a feud, fathers often get
their young sons to do the deed for them.
If a grown Turk kills, he may be hanged;
but a boy goes to reform school
and learns a trade,
training hands that did the other job
to also make clean boots.

7.

O poets of Anatolia
why do you imagine golden birds?
Do you not see how your heroes
sing with a sword?

8.

The sand is moving.
A massacre is about to occur.

9.

It is night all day. Shadowed killers
rouse sleepers to blood and death.
The swordsman straddles the dismembered limbs.

10.

At the sight of these men
moving in a green army
even the summits of Ararat
cry out, cry out.

11.

I too am now remembering
the massacres of the Armenians.
My mind whirls like Rumi's.
I too am a spinning dervish
who dreams of union with God
unlike the historic swordsman
who is an adept,
his whirling not a show for tourists.

12.

In the *hammam* dank and dark,
he blooms;
his wet body
a steam-kissed pink flower,
chest anointed,
legs polished
by stones from a river
whose far-off water
sounds drowned chimes for corpses.

13.

About 1915.
I know old griefs
for lucid inescapable reasons.
But I know, too, the denial.
Yes, Anatolia's denial
is involved
in what I know.

OTHER REVELATIONS

First Revelation

They should have been buried in ice or peat.
The spirit would remember the body perfectly:

how this woman once called to her son
while stuffing vine leaves with nuts and rice –

how this girl flashed eyes at this boy
(her neck slashed, his right arm sundered) –

how this old man prayed
while flames ate his flesh in the church pyre –

how this mother, with the bayonet inside her,
would have loved this baby in her belly

calling his name to the stars
dancing in the night sky –

how this child, newly born, its brains decorating rock,
would have loved Beethoven, imagining a moonlight sonata.

Their memories could have been revelations,
their passions a validation of imagination.

Their murders are a statistic, not these metaphors.
Their spirits are encoded in air currents and river sediment.

Second Revelation

Up to their knees in death, the murderers go on
killing with an insistence on being perfect.

Each slaughter is prefaced with prayer –
fanaticism is a pristine religion.

They see the sweet salt blood
running all the way to Damascus

and they laugh in ecstasy
at pyramids of flesh
covering bone-pits
sad jewels of the dead.

Third Revelation

Under the Euphrates
are minarets of skulls
filigreed with last thoughts
into which fishes glide.

From Angora to Zeitun,
the A to Z of sudden history,
generations vanishing in a wilderness
blinded by locust wings.

For those who survived
it is the end of cosmos:

Absurd heroic survivors
rewarded with nightmares

of how easily we are overcome,
how cleverly destroyed.

IT IS TRUE...

It is true you knock on a door;
no answer because
it's an Armenian house
where no one has lived for almost a century.

It is true...
you go to their museums
expecting some truth
about the massacres, but find
the story turned the other way around.

Your mind rejects their version
to preserve your soul
and you shroud yourself in silence
to muffle the knowing:
you will be dismissed as an unbeliever.

It is true...
they espouse a fear of Allah
and a love for the Koran's beauty,
especially the chapter on Heavenly Light,
and you wonder how this
fits their history and the genocide denied.

It is true...
today you want them
to acknowledge these crimes,
to make peace with civilization.
But waves of noise and motion are overwhelming,
as if from the doors of toilets
comes the whiff of corpses.

PART THREE:
EVEN THE MOST BROKEN LIFE

☀

THE ANGELS OF ARSHILE GORKY

Angels battled over him
in the village under a bluff.
His village with its name, a double syllable,
portending somewhere deep, stable.

Angel of birth carries a sheep
like a child, tethers it to a post
for a wolf to tear and carry in its teeth.
       Angel of death
       brings self-destruction.

GORKY'S TRUE NAME

In new syllables Arshile Gorky unravels –
a foreign scroll welcoming new modes, new moods,
the old names dropping into a far-off chasm,
unholy vanishing point.

New names tremble on a cliff edge,
facing flame, surging water, molten rock.
What moves beneath is a sea
gathering for a catastrophe.

His eyes go deeper than his name
into horror – picturing monsters
and delirium – nothing transcendent
about his staggering illness.

GORKY IN PHOTOS AND DRAWINGS

There is a hanged man in his face,
despair presaged from childhood
in Khorkhom, where every family
had orphans who battled demons
and terrors from birth.
Eyes the colour of coal,
bitter eyes that saw faces
practising the *bastinado*.
Eyes that memorized his mother's
wild stare when she remembered
her young first husband's murder.
Eyes that saw in *Guernica*
the obscenities in Van.

Hands were a different story,
decorating eggs at Easter,
drawing fish on sand, working with wood,
engraving silver, mending shoes,
painting arabesques in long sweeps,
and throttling anyone who fanned his rage.

But he draws only his face in black,
lines rather than planes,
rubbing the pastel, making shadows
of mad melancholy.
The eyes are alert, stare right through you;
above them, the brows are vulture wings.
If he tilted his face down,
they would hover over valleys of carrion,
the face of a man expecting death by his own hand,
because the torment is always
rooted in earth.

ARSHILE GORKY, WHILE PAINTING

He is thinking flame, cigarette dangling
from his mouth, thin lines of paint
weaving red plumes. Light falls
in beams, silver tilting
from the glass-eyed window.
Each broad stroke of brush –
an ember glow. It is unfinished still.
He never wants to say
"complete" or "it is done."
The thing to do: Always
add paint to paint, not with sadness
because there's joy in twisting the devil.
In a corner, a wood stove snaps and pops,
fire hissing deep satisfaction, logs
quivering like bones on a pyre.

Heat moves his mind to the past,
oven in the floor of a mud-house
by Lake Van, inland sea.
Family oven where coal vanishes,
tribes seeing the world vanish,
skins afflicted like dark hides of oxen.
Villages picked clean, trails of dropped bodies,
children and women shocked in sunless caves
ignited at the end of nothing.
Lost to red tongues licking at their skin,
they hope for retreat to the sea,
choosing blue as their last colour,
a mercy to give them possible existence,
surprise of survival in a berserk world.

He paces back and forth, mind stoking fire
for an art of fate, sketches
of the dead hidden in black lines,
no absolute but the absolute of ruins.

His figures have no faces, but are evidence
they endure. Eyes which have seen
sparks of intention, infinite affliction,
dying bodies which parse torture,
broken will. Such figures outlive us all,
even when their hands hold nothing,
not even the shape of fingers.
His burden is the act of remembering
burials, witnessing those who sit
near fire, feeling close to fire,
making a truce with ordinary flame.

He, too, feels a kinship with embers,
the sudden swagger of inferno.

Flame is his grandmother Hamaspiur
beating at the church door, screaming grief
for a son's body carved with daggers,
then giving God a nightmare
in her madness, setting the nave aflame
with a loose match cast into darkness.

What matters is the heat beyond despair,
what matters is the dead made memorable –
eyes and mouths open, knives in their hearts,
lives flowing their lava to an enormous sea.

GORKY'S MOTHER

His excited brush paints surface
as metaphor, mirror for what is seen
or half-seen. Something felt in homage
and atonement so she will not vanish
in an unmarked grave.

The easel is her pedestal, his shades
of rose and terracotta are relics of the pink
tufa of Aghtamar, Armenian earth
and stone.
      Fearful she'll be lost to oblivion,
he restores her to life, standing as a boy
beside her, every brush stroke breathing benisons
and the quick spirit of a Madonna.

GORKY'S DRAWING OF BOY AND HORSE

freehand in pencil
which lasts longer than the hand
of a boy in love with shapes
of natural tenderness.

the same hand
that grows to feed
grapes to his beloved.

the hand that will hold his firstborn
as he whispers its name to the stars.

the hand that cracks its anger
across faces and paints emptiness.

the hand that will throw a rope
across a beam to hang the future
man in the boy who loved horses.

NIGHTTIME, ENIGMA, AND NOSTALGIA (1931-33)

1.

The Picasso of Washington Square,
the old master
running in his fingertips.
A susceptibility to influence
sometimes made him anxious,
but leaders were impressive,
placing him in the long line
of history. As the son, he could not
kill his artist father.

2.

He kept his objects whole
with brush strokes, placing
them in flat planes, fruits
and vegetables morphing into ears,
an eye, a leg – animation
of a Protean palette
stopping at the canvas edge.

3.

Always connected to an inner
life. Colours could dazzle
before the murders in Khorkhom, then
darken into night, a pencil
surgically taking out the light,
lines pulsing a visceral passion
from hand to paper.

Matisse and Ingres taught him lines,
clean, delicate, looping, so his hand
never had to leave the paper,
a lover clinging to a partner,
sensitive to emotional nuance.

4.

Not merely a niggling craft,
stroke by measured stroke, but
an obsession with forms free of bravado.
He rubbed and splashed,
washed away inspiration or made
grooves and indentations, scraping
white from black like the metalwork
of childhood, a black liquorice
to savour in pen and china ink.

5.

The melancholy of nostalgia
even in peeled bodies a year before,
torn off, muscles and tendons exposed,
sound of bones coming to his ears.
A magical musculature swirling
metamorphic, as calf muscles
turn into birds, the flayed
figure a bird head, its backbone
reaching upward
like a rope from which
a hanged man dangles.

6.

Meandering lines within a trapezoid,
linear web breeding permutations
of contrasting bio-morphs.
A wide-eyed female wrestling
a contorted male in nocturnal gloom,
a sad musing on enigma –
the puzzle of sex, his wrestling
with Sirun, wild mare of high-bred

energy. He painted at night, squeezing
ochre out of tubes in long snakes,
stroking the canvas with a palette knife,
some strokes thick, some delicate,
his breathing calibrated to the moving hand.
Sex was romance in the head, energy
saved for art or hysterical explosions
to tame Sirun the Armenian way
so he would hold her image forever
enthralled to his worship.

7.

Drawing on paper, with eyes inside
loops. Pictures could have vision
to look into his soul. His ink
washed over them, the eyes
surviving brown water
he rubbed with a damp cloth
as if paper were skin.
When he studied them, eyes
were the look of his people,
time swirling around their martyrdom,
his nostalgia for darkness
a cavernous solitude.

8.

Anxiety and depression at bay,
not loneliness. His studio
pitch-dark at noon,
the hallway painted black
so he could open his door just a crack
without being seen. Heavy furniture
with solid legs. Three straight-backed
chairs to punish intruders. Scrubbed
parquet floors the colour of sand.
A spareness to match solitude
for a nomad used to struggle.
He always had to put up
with himself.

9.

At Union Square, the homeless
wrapped in newspapers
and in dismembered cardboard boxes.
In Central Park, a wounded pigeon
about to drown in a pond swollen
with new rain. The bird's agony
bred the melancholy of his special models:
"Wounded birds, poverty,
and one whole week of rain."

10.

Nighttime, enigma, nostalgia.
Look again. Strange forms float
on a shallow black surface,
curve penetrating curve.
Behind the cross-hatched precision
and flatness hangs
          a remembered world
beyond reality "where once
the great centuries danced."

ELEGY FOR WILLIAM SAROYAN

Always a lunatic running around inside his head,
but his plays were a sweet miracle's making,
places to lick malignancies in himself
and bet on tomorrow morning.

Decades of loud-mouthed celebration
because in the time of his life, he had to live –
and laugh in his thick, bristling moustache
at the mystery and delight of it
so he could drown out the silence.

To be a man was a family thing, his meaning.
His heart in the highlands, on a trapeze
or quietly crying under comedy
for remembered bodies mummifying
in Bitlis.

Lived in his own gut, a rabble-rouser's
pomposa voice, before the rages
cut off his children, jars of twigs, coins,
buttons in the background – things that could
flower or glint.

Pain was humiliating, disease
a final reminder the world was
a big fat falsehood, after all,
and he had no time left
for slippery forgiveness.

LITURGY FOR SAROYAN

That Christ drank vinegar at the Last Supper,
that we ate glass, so blood would fall
from our mouths, would juice our wounds.

That he was chosen to praise
the grace of strangers, their sweet madness.
That he would learn from wild flowers,

and the traces of a stone house.
That Bitlis was his monument of loss.
That he had the feeling to reclaim it.

That he could stop mourning.
That, in the end, he could not forget.
That he would learn there is no love

separate from heartbreak.
That he could not afford emotional needs,
that he hadn't been able to since he was three.

That he could not afford to be grateful –
for even gratitude would be a need.
That he dared say to God:

Why do you give Armenians so little
to thank you for?

PARADJANOV

1.

His camera paints
by tableaux, a steady gaze
locked in light, iconic
romance of the mind.

He frames the real with absolute care,
servant of gestures complete
yet mysterious, geometry of composition
a meticulous habit, refusing
the commissars' dictates, the tyranny
of their stifling literalness.
The shock of his freedom
is luminous in Tbilisi.

2.

His burdens are other people's lives,
the difficult, grievous, betrayed
gossip of voyeurs, outcries
of madonnas, plainness of children,
the sorcerer's stratagems,
everyone on the same long road,
but "those who walk and those who ride
cannot be companions."

3.

The minstrel's lute floats down a stream
not sinking, a sign it is pure and blessed.
Sometimes only the wind brings songs
for harvest dances and marriage rituals,
air piping through birches,
rice spilling on pomegranates,
his mind dreaming
shadows of forgotten ancestors.

4.

Life is merely a visitation
to islands where God is needed
even if He is feared.

Sometimes life is brutal:
Storm clouds cascade black milk
in a sorcerer's malignant magic.
Yet dreams turn storms away,
bring withered lilies back to life.

His camera eye peers
into the mysteries of water –
rivers running out of books,
ponds with tentacled reeds
snaring a cross of vine
fastened with Saint Nino's hair lock.
Everything disappears and everything
remains in his universe.

Time waxes with wisdom
as a candle burns out.
The raucous feast is done,
the dancers poised in early morning mist,
birds in quiet convocation,
horses munching fallen apples.
He catches the morning flare
as if it were his final day.

5.

La Giaconda weeps in his art,
black days flap like foul butterflies,
and bread baked in his mother's bosom
sours in his universe's tears.

Yet everything lies ahead of everything.
Art, not pain alone, inhabits him.
Imagination calls for truth
incandescent with the flame of desire.

Our hurts are painful to the soul:
Siberia, barbed wire, isolation.
Ghosts persist: mother, father, childhood,
home defiled, the hearth invaded by *djinns*.

Phantoms have nowhere to go except to Paradjanov.
Fifteen years of lonely idleness later,
he knows he is going to die,
giving his genius to Armenia.

THOUGHTS ON PARADJANOV'S
THE COLOUR OF POMEGRANATES

Pomegranates die on white tablecloths,
their blood spilling
in a world where we search
for ourselves in one another.

Stones squeeze water from books,
our mouths moving like fish
over the running pages.

We learn the world, only to leave it.

Poet with hennaed palms, blood cross
on his forehead – inside him
a great song is hiding.

His heart fills with snow
trampled by a beloved's feet.

Silence in this vast moment
before the sound of affliction
happening again and again.

The self persists, though the heart
is trampled like a grape,
and we are exiled from love.

The song alone does not desert us,
we whose lives and souls
are tortured.

ON SEEING EGOYAN'S *CALENDAR*

To the sound of flute song and drum:
the pastoral begins on the mountain road,
an unending flock of sheep (coarse tufted)
carries us along to a sad story
about churches and calendars.
There is an energy in each place
that goes beyond beauty.
Nothing is accidental: the sky
and the church refuse chance.

Seeing a cluster of brown turrets on a hill,
we ask: *What does it mean when you hear our story?*
And stones pocked by centuries shape a mute chorus.
Come closer, stranger. Touch
and feel how we are constructed,
well composed, naturally lit, seductive.
These places make us strangers,
remind us we have forgotten
ancestral dreams.

We are *from here, but being here*
has made us
from somewhere else.

What is the best image for what we know –
turrets and the people who made that history?
A church and fortress in ruins release our musing:
All that is meant to protect us
is bound to fall apart,
bound to become contrived, useless and absurd.
All that's meant to protect is bound to isolate, and
all that's meant to isolate is bound to hurt.

EGOYAN'S ARCHIVES OF INTIMACY

Private nightmares: lampshades
of human skin, skull ashtrays,
scalps.

Films collect images too, packing archives:
a father who tapes over videos of his family
with pornography, and a son who erases both;
a mausoleum of speaking video;
a photographer of Armenian churches;
the customs officer collecting baggage tags,
then drawing their owners' faces from memory;
a cool psychopath hoarding cooking-show videos
and women's bodies.

Archives can access intimacy, even depression.

Outside, things collapse.

AFTER VIEWING *ARARAT*

A husband can return after slipping
over a cliff, someone you missed
in the middle of a sentence.
A father can be held in a spool of film
making you witness the atrocity
that claimed him. Another emerges
from the darkness of old books,
endless histories which return facts from graves,
words holding the scent of blood.
Books which say: Go wherever you want
but always return to now.

The room is blanched by daylight.
His father's ghost comes to Gorky
as he paints his mother and the boy
who is himself, holding small flowers –
a gift to his absent father.
This painting saves his mother from oblivion,
snatching her from a pile of corpses
to put her on a pedestal.

Even the most broken life can be
reclaimed in such moments. Believing
you can see Ararat from a window
in Van (although you cannot),
because it is yours, and you must
dream of a way to make it belong
to you always, belong to the child
you were, to the child you became.
The painting, the mountain, a repository
of who you are. A sacred code
which is really about love and survival –
first love running through fields, heaven in your eyes
and summer without end. Not expecting nails
through your heel of skin and bone, nor

your young lover's bare-breasted dance in a circle,
urged by whips, bodies anointed
by kerosene, a fragrance sweeter
than honey, and the living, who re-play
the torture, crying in trauma: "How
shall we tear out our eyes?"

You are part of all this, and must know
what causes the most pain
is neither the kin you lost nor the land.
It is knowing you could be hated
and now are hated even more,
as the sky leaves signatures of cloud
and nothing else − only blue hours
and your desperate need to be remembered.

Snowy Ararat and sky.
There's nothing here to prove anything,
but you must return to the mountain
to put something back into your heart,
find a way to remember what you need to remember.
You are more vulnerable when you lose meaning,
although meaning changes, along with remembrance.
Like the invisible mother in Edward Saroyan's
back story, you eat one pomegranate seed a day,
pretending it is the whole fruit
to bring luck and the power to imagine
what you cannot remember.

PART FOUR:
OUR BURDENS AND OUR
HISTORIES

❖

POPPIES

Their deep dye changes
voluptuous fields to red
beautiful with love
or so the Persians said.

In heat or drought
they have made a world
where sleep can come
in anxious soil.

They grow reveries
for a homeland,
deep red sleep
in a harrowed place.

They breathe dreams
into communion with air,
their seeds astonishing
by their power to endure.

INDOCTRINATION OF A TURKISH BOY

Tell him how history has losers and victors.
Tell him they are bitter in defeat.
Don't tell him about fabrication.

Tell him it's important to be quiet.
Tell him skeletons in the photographs are Jews.
Don't tell him they are Armenians.

Tell him they were people who hated Turks.
Tell him the same thing repeatedly.
Don't tell him about their convulsive misery.

Tell him they were a disgrace.
Tell him they were a curse.
Don't tell him how they became fossils.

Tell him everything was done for their own good.
Tell him the screams were of angry birds.
Don't tell him about the clubs, axes, knives.

Tell him they were moved from inhospitable lands.
Tell him they were sent to where they could prosper.
Don't tell him about the canyons, caves, or desert.

Tell him the statistics are skewed.
Tell him it's their strategy of resourceful recollection.
Don't tell him the unpleasant truths.

Tell him you'll say more when the time comes.
Tell him this is not the time to re-visit history.

Don't tell him you select what you want to remember.

Don't tell him anything more.

DENYING HISTORY

Some liars make a network
electric with conspiracy
controlling the circuit
recharging the lies
ritualizing the repetition
of an old script –

energy of the empowered
infiltrating every raw sound,
impressing a presence
by the crafty blurring of fact.

The will to avert one's face
from the lingering mausoleum:
its burden of anonymous bodies,
the pornography of cruelty
no one could imagine
with a naked mind.

Denial haunts with ferocious rigour,
the audacity to look you in the face
while shredding the truth,
undercutting your ground of pain.

You will find no refuge in the future's arms.

ELEGY FOR ARMENIA

1.

I have only pieces of Armenia
in my mind, assembling them
to resemble an optic heart
I want to keep forever –

traces of the befallen,
importune remembrance,
lost moments of love
I can count in melancholy.

Blood surges in my ears
as the leaves fall,
a scattering of gold barely
moving into sound.

This silence is holy,
having rights to invisible meaning
I must make real as names
we desire to keep forever –
if forever could transcend ghosts
disappearing, then living again in me.

How lightning accompanies love
in the heart,
amazement of fire and tears,
a thundering crackle
while I call out my kinship
with ghosts of the befallen.

2.

Neither words nor truths are enough,
brave and strong, against killers
mad to insist the real doesn't exist,
who say that the slaughtered died
owing to obscure interests
for which the dead must be blamed.

The crimes built in waves
surging across fields
of leaves waxing colour,
then waning, nature revised,
twigs and branches
gesturing out of dry silence.

3.

Mounds of desecration,
abodes of the dead
truly gone into grounds of the real.

There is no map for the chambers
of stilled hearts, pulped brains,
topography of the deceased.

Black birds of fate descend
offering songs no other birds sing,
voices erasing silence above
figures turned to dust,
traces of the undeniable dead.

I have walked these fields
in all seasons, feet keeping time
with elegy, time my vaporous
guide, bidding me remember:
language, heart-like,
never neutral.

Here was life
tasted on the tongue, voluptuous
and resolute, before the malicious
horizon forced the spine's unravelling.

Over a million lives
driven across terror,
bodies choking caves and rivers.

History only hears the forsaken
when poets are born from atrocity,
making words from massive debris
of a race trapped between
Never Was and Does Not Exist.

4.

What to do with a place of absence?
Nostalgia does not help. The gulf
between ourselves and the voiceless dead
grows by generations. The grass becomes
votive, insects hopping pulses,
killers and the killed joined in oblivion.

Sometimes truth cannot speak itself
according to the shape of ache
as real as atoms or dead stars
of a smashed multitude.

Every time has its wisdom,
but what is ours? Will it come
on civilized feet, or smash
like a fist through wood –
passion free of delicacy
to pivot an avenging angel?

Anger burns my face
flaming moral questions
where everything has fallen:

Apples from the bough,
plums in their pregnant sacs,
pomegranates whose cells
are poisoned by arid winds
storming like chariots.

Nothing will be green again.

THIS TONGUE TRIES

The stars stay awake all night,
turning, turning in their bruised light.

Mothers speak to me in dreams,
telling of swarms of mayhem.

Galaxies of women float in a sea of dreams –
half are really nightmares.

No relief from the body or reconstruction of the mind.
More than a century of long silence.

Imagine this silence as the burning of books,
a library sending signals of smoke.

Yet a few words in an age of combustion
are traced by my hand against the swagger of flame.

This tongue tries a reparation of speech
beyond the reliquary ashes of books.

It licks the caves where the dead
lie in their long hibernation.

How offensive my words seem, powerless
against the eye's obscenities.

And how this concrete, unforgiving world, now and then,
writhes, gripped in the thick jaws of monsters.

WHAT FOLLOWS WORDS

Words are not the world,
never are solutions —
only a gauze for wounded civilization.

Should I fall silent, paralyzed
by the emptiness of words,
break apart like Holderlin
in a "radiance of the inexpressible"?

Or drown
in Paul Celan's Seine,
having written the past
and left the vital unwritten?

What is left to say about Adana
that Belsen left unsaid
at the bitter edge of silence?

PLATES

White poppies on a blue porcelain background,
snowy Ararat in the distance – these plates
are gestural ghosts of glazed mortality
that sadden the landscape.

Spared by the assassins, they lie chipped with weeds
in empty courtyards, where dirt and air
retain, a century later, leavings
of waking days and nights.

History, in porcelain retrospection, gleans
something of black beds or gardens
where savage feet had trampled lives,
ground spattered with fallen cries.

This is a sorcerer's imagination.

Reality is tangled in terrible truths:
Wolves howling at the moon,
pestilence in orange groves,
the beast in man stealing his soul.

Years they have lain there, plates and history,
finding a random sanctuary:
        Porcelain poetry
where death and memory go together.

These plates speak against death.
What endures is brittle blue porcelain
transfixing time, defying chaos
and nothingness.

PERSPECTIVE

Always the same:
The bandit Armenian
versus the poor traduced Turk.
It was a civil war, you see,
not a genocide – a few infidels
to be sacrificed
for a pure empire.

And they were patriots too,
who died heroically.

No death march, just a re-location.

No rape, starvation, or murder,
just sheer bad luck and cholera
befalling the unbelievers.

The good and the merciful
granted the traitors release –

and oblivion.

A HISTORY OF ARMENIA

for Lorne Shirinian

Always a flight from relics,
stone crosses cut
with pomegranates and grapes,
a tale of abrupt parting
without words of comfort.

A tale of fissures and fission
continuing. Goodbyes
from the dock, train station,
dusty pathways. Hearts uprooted.
Children watching, Eden only a myth.

Dispersion. A rite of movement,
specimens of Armenia transplanted:
Armenian Kitchen. Ararat Bakery.
An illuminated manuscript in classical Armenian
in a Toronto library. Rug merchants
in Oakville, Guelph, Burlington,
their brushed carpets in vegetable dyes opening a new world.

Those who search for orchards, white walls,
and filigreed roofs of family homes search
to prove their own presence.

Between Van and Moscow,
between Cyprus and San Francisco,
between London and Fresno,
we are in-between, wanting to get on with living.

Every family repeats the same story
to get closer to the truth.
They leave Armenia
to discover Armenia
everywhere.

ISTANBUL IN DARKNESS, GRIEVING

Houses, streets, ghettoes of childhood.
The world almost forgetting these existed.
Your city has always hidden its ruins,
its black bile, its melancholy.

Cities, like families, expect love and luck
the way lovers do
in the acceptance of bodies, in their imperfections.

We live in different fantasies of the same museum:
bric-à-brac, photographs, locked glass cabinets,
silent pianos, beaded curtains, large heavy carpets,
and an old nanny who can no longer read love letters
from a dead suitor.

Outside the semi-darkness of these relics,
the streets are weary, light declining
on the surfaces of fallen down mansions,
crowds huddled in winter's thick coat,
night rubbing its cold into streets and lives.
Battered streetlamps, old wooden houses,
concrete apartments, chiaroscuro of decay.

Age, neglect, dirt, and humidity
confuse the tourist's eye,
misinterpreting the value of the colour black.
Dark haze on smoky mornings
settles on rooftops or in eaves and gardens
left untended – not the pretty tints of etchings
painted by foreign hands.

Darkness is a cover for the eye
peering at ghosts and shadows. Darkness makes
a moral point. This darkness
a grieving for what has fallen into ruin.

WHERE ARE THE ARMENIANS IN ISTANBUL?

What are the covered women at remote bus stops thinking
as they clutch their groceries and speak to no one?
Are they reflecting on emptiness –
boathouses of old, disused villas,
unemployed men in teahouses, pimps
on summer evenings awaiting drunken tourists,
broken seesaws in vacant parks, shame-faced men
in porno cinemas, holy messages – letters missing –
between minarets, clock towers no one notices,
girls vending cut-rate meat?

Do they think of everything broken,
worn-out, and of the *hüzün?* A persistent heartache
in the remains of a mighty empire? A *hüzün* that rises
like shame in old eyes? *Istanbulis*, you claim this melancholy is not
     illness but choice. You are half right.
The denied past removes dignity, enlarges shame.

There is no honour, no relief in denial.
Return the word "Armenian" to Turkey.
The word with many ghosts.

"Genocide" would be accurate, more truthful –
but for now you may use it
only in exile.

THE NEED FOR PRECISION

One apple plus one apple make two
without dissent. The mathematics
of apples can make for certitude.
Some particles of matter
count more than bodies
where the losses are not exact, where
the lost are a loss in meaning,
indeterminate spectres flitting
across maps.

In an inventory of claim, how easy
to account for clay bowls,
for gall-nut, sugar and rice,
hemp cords and silk clothes.
The tally of torts worth gold.
But where is the precision
of headless bodies, of unmarked graves,
shreds of scarves hanging in walnut trees,
of apple-cheeked children
whose golden hair was carried
by winds to the mountains?

THE MURDER OF HRANT DINK

It is a story, Hrant,
repeated for generations,
a long story that keeps
happening over and over,
growing in the telling until you reach
the edge of the world,
tracked down while the sun cries out
against you, and darkness swallows the day,
and suddenly there's silence, while you keep running
within yourself in the grim trespass of pain.

Your killers turn you into a sacrifice –
something special which becomes sacred,
incandescent against deniers
who devour their nation.

Your body in the street, after threats and trials
cannot break you –
bleeds fear of what else might happen.
And the mourners cry out your name
with love and despair, having come
to see your body,
the story itself and not simply its name –
and they call out your name over and over again,
wanting to identify with you:

They are all Hrant Dink.
I am, too.

I, WHO HAVE NOT ASCENDED ARARAT

but looked into the ruins of Nineveh
and felt the splash of the tears of Araxes
would write Armenia

in every Turkish history book, in every
school where revisionism is the new barbarity
(second genocide), inject Armenian blood
back into the veins of Abdul Hamid,
whose mother died from slow consumption
and her husband's raw pathology.
I would bring back the maps of the Bible,
bring back the Armenian schools,
bring back the guidebooks where Armenians
haunt ruined churches with memories
of ethnic cleansing.

Let the voice of Taner Akcam ring clear
so the sick man of Europe may rise
and be healed.

ADAM'S FINAL TRUTH

So rare was his warm touch on my head or skin
I cannot remember it, the waters of childhood
turning murky with faults, foam receding
from toes in sand as I watched him battle
the waves, a feeling of things shrinking
away from me underfoot. He was powerful
then, his muscled body glistening,
his legs contesting currents. I thought
for a while he was the strongest man
in the world, one who could tame the sea,
command the beach, own a kingdom.
He was a romance – his body
magnified, separating light
from darkness, forcing water
to swallow defeat.

Cancer shrank him in old age.
I was not with him when death came
in the municipal hospital, his lips
parched, the intravenous drip silent,
moonlight grim upon the window.
He died in his sleep, unable to reach
for water on the table, unable to gasp out
his plague of thirst. His mouth
a small black hole, caught
with grotesque suddenness
in the *rigor mortis* of unspoken
havoc. It locked open
in a silent, parched cry.

A strong man shrunk
into the final truth of mortality.
How small his emaciated body seemed,
its bones and shrivelled skin
relics of an ultimate
abandonment.

But he has grown
in me as I stir memory's water:
His story from another century
bearing me with it, washing away
darkness, despair, devastation,
yet leaving the face
of a dead man, diminished
in body, and a dry ground
for reconciliation –
his shadow in the grave,
and a pain greater
than pain, immeasurable
distance from here
to heaven, unforgivable.

THEIR MEMORIES BURN

1.

They didn't know their race had failures
or the odour of garlic that made them unclean.
Like devout Jews, they thought themselves special,
their eyes able to see many things
as yet undestroyed by fire:

feast day smiles and sugar cubes,
hopscotch that children marked with chalk,
bread and salt on snow-white tablecloths –
hospitality for strangers –
fruit describing geometry in glazed bowls,
wine warming bodies without burning them down.

2.

They thought they knew their limits
for possible perfection.

But the spirits that passed over their homes
were exterminating angels

leaving spinning tops to wobble to a standstill,
milk to sour in dwindling pantries,

sepia to run like old sores
out of family photos

and new heat waves to come —
flames feeding on

what they had seen,
glistening, growing in devouring torsion.

They were forced to breathe differently
in the blowtorch melting of things.

Their memories burn in me like yellow flames.

DENIAL – AN AFTERWORD

DENIAL – AN AFTERWORD

I am a swimmer in most waters, but my father's people sank into the burning Tigris as if sucked down by whirlpools.

Truth must learn to buoy itself up, or drown in tides of historical denial.

On the night of April 24, 1915, the Ottoman Government rounded up and imprisoned an estimated 250 Armenian intellectuals and community leaders in Trabzon. The Armenians included lawyers, merchants, bankers, teachers, clergymen, newspaper editors, composers, translators, chemists, physicists, theatre directors, playwrights, restaurant owners, an official interpreter for the deputy British Consul in Constantinople, and others.

In the same year, Turkish authorities in Trabzon herded thousands of Armenian women and children onto boats and drowned them in the Black Sea.

We cannot pretend that Trabzon is irrelevant to the responsible life of the imagination and hence to poetry.

Darkness had fallen from the air.

We cannot say for sure if the men who devised and fulfilled Trabzon, Adana, Harput, Van, Zeitung, etc., had been taught to read poetry. Therefore, we cannot say if they could ask themselves what they were really about as human beings. We cannot say that they could even have understood the question.

"Others had to write the poetry of ruin," says George Steiner. "Ruin is the starting point of any serious thought about literature."

"The carcass of the rotting dog cannot speak for you," wrote Leonard Cohen. "The ovens have no tongue." But his tongue spoke against the smokestacks of Auschwitz long after Nazi denial. In this way, the word survives mere fact. In this way, the word survives history and anti-history.

Denial seeks to set limits to what can be spoken. Those who perpetrated 1915 sought to deny it. As have their descendants.

After a lecture on the Armenian genocide by Ara Sarafian and Vincent Lima at Drexel University, Philadelphia, a Turkish sympathizer asked mockingly: "What were Armenians doing before the so-called Genocide? Were they sitting at home singing songs?"

Trabzon's governor declared to Reuter's Gareth Jones, who was investigating the murder of Hrant Dink, that the crime was related to "social problems linked to urbanization." He suggested that "A strong gun culture and the fiery character of the people" might be to blame.

A March 2006 symposium in Turkey on Armenian-Turkish relations yielded the following claims: "Deportation was a means of crisis management" and "The death toll of deportation is comparable to the death toll of the flu epidemic in England at the time."

A choice of words can divide truth from denial.
Sometimes denial can be made through reticence. Robert Fisk's *The Great War for Civilization* was published in Turkish "quietly," i.e., without press coverage or reviews in Turkey. His massive book has a chapter on "The First Holocaust".

❈ ❈ ❈

It's absurd to expect an apology from people who have not been told it happened.
     (Atom Egoyan)

For the Armenians, time was a cycle in which the
past incarnated in the present and the present birthed
the future. For the Turks, time was a multi-hyphenated
line, where the past ended at some definite point
and the present started anew from scratch, and there
was nothing but rupture in between.
(Elif Shafak, *The Bastard of Istanbul*)

A French-born writer of Turkish descent and an award-winning
novelist who also teaches in the U.S., Ms. Shafak was accused by
nationalist lawyers of insulting Turkish identity in her novel. The
charges were later dropped.

The past can be too much of a burden, so we deny it.

On December 15, 2005, a gang of Azeri desecrators in
Azerbaijan used sledgehammers, cranes, and trucks to destroy
thousands of pink and red headstones (*kchackars*) in a medieval
Armenian graveyard in remote, windswept Djulfa. In what was
the largest Armenian cemetery in the world, pieces of stone lay
like bones in the mud.

This is a denial that can tolerate no testimony against it.

The genocide was banishment from life. Denial turns genocide
into banishment from death.

Living with denial, lies never die.

Denial is also blindness, a self-mutilation, as if the burden of
guilt had nowhere to escape except through eyes that must, then,
be veiled or shut in shame. This is how eyes become as blind as
stone.

In 1930, Wittgenstein maintained: "Words can only describe things of which we can form mental pictures."

A human object of hate has something projected onto him or her: a mental picture of what he or she represents to enemies.

Article 305 of the Turkish Penal Code forbids the use of the term "genocide" to describe the events of 1915. In 1975, historian Taner Akcam was arrested for writing that there are Kurds in Turkey. In 1991, Leyla Zana, the first Kurdish woman elected to the Turkish Parliament, took her oath of office in Kurdish, a language banned in the country. Three years later, she was arrested and charged with treason. In 2006, Orhan Pamuk was charged with insulting "Turkishness" by talking about the mass murders of Kurds and Armenians. There are, of course, "no Kurds in Turkey," and it is considered perverse to believe that the Armenian genocide ever happened.

Historical revisionism is tense with effort. It cuts across religions and cultures, thriving on equal opportunity. In 1997, the Palestine Ministry of Information claimed that a century's work of archaeological excavations in the Old City of Jerusalem found no tangible evidence of any Jewish traces or remains there. *Ergo*, there was no Jerusalem the ways Jews claim there was.

Historical revisionism is also a problem with words. The Israeli government, under Ariel Sharon, attempted to remove even marginal references to the Nakba (cataclysm) from Israeli textbooks. The catastrophe of mass deportation, massacres of civilians, and destruction of villages of thousands of Palestinians during the 1948 Arab-Israeli War had become a shame it was necessary to conceal. It was a shame reaching back to the position of Zionist extremists, such as Israel Zangvil, who described Zionists as "a people without land returning to a land without people" – a statement that turned Palestinians into temporary landholders and hence a non-existent factor, as far as the success story of the Jewish state was concerned.

Bishop Richard Williamson spent years denying the Shoah, culminating in his statement on Swedish television in January 2009: "I believe there were no gas chambers." He added that only [*sic*] up to 300,000 Jews were killed in Nazi camps. A week later, just days before the annual international Holocaust Memorial Day (the anniversary of the liberation of Auschwitz), Pope Benedict XVI rescinded the bishop's excommunication from the Roman Catholic Church.

Denial bears an international passport. It taints every nation: the United States (Hiroshima, Nagasaki, Vietnam, Cambodia, and Iraq), Canada (racial and sexual abuse of First Nations children in residential schools, or its treatment of Japanese Canadians during World War II – all acknowledged only recently in Parliament), Australia ("stolen generations"), England, Japan, China, Russia, Africa, India, Pakistan, etc. Too many hands are steeped in blood – sometimes over pigmentation or a circumcised foreskin.

Historical revisionism can be a forgery. Even the words "Catastrophe", "Calamity", and "Tragedy" become forgeries, because they are used like cheap imitations of the real events. They shift the names of things and therefore alter whatever was reality.

❋ ❋ ❋

Reality is not. It must be searched for and won.
    (Paul Celan)

Celan compared poetry to a message in a bottle that is thrown out to sea in the hope that one day it will wash ashore, "perhaps on the shore of the heart."

In my 1970s poem "Armenian Elegy," I wrote (long before I ever knew of or read Celan):

> History is a colophon:
> shipwrecked words stuffed in bottles
> drifting   get help soon
> to no one.

I now understand my own metaphor in the light of Celan's explanation:

> Poems even in this sense are under way; they are
> heading toward something. Toward what? Toward some
> open place that can be inhabited, toward a thou which
> can be addressed, perhaps toward a reality which can be
> addressed.

Denial can hurt a writer into poetry, but the poet need not disappear so much into imagination as to be absent from the real world. There is a place to bear witness to a devastation of grace and to some hope beyond despair.

> A tree-
> high thought
> strikes the note of light: there are
> still songs to sing beyond
> mankind.
>   (Paul Celan)

In my prose memoir *Pain: Journeys Around My Parents* (2000) I wrote:

> Many Armenians of the older generations have a saying:
> "When the past is behind you, keep it there." But this is
> a gesture of defeat in an age that promotes denial. This
> way the intrusive past cannot be channelled; this way
> Isaiah can be silenced in the void from where he would
> cry, "Truly Thou art a God Who Hides Himself."

An Armenian phrase that I value suggests the past is invoked in snatches: *Djamangeen gar oo chagar.* "A long time ago, there was and there wasn't." Our human insecurity and doubt can be comforted by lyric memory, though only partially filling the void.

Memory is poisoned by denial. We have the right to dream that denial will run to its own ruin. That one day a true mental picture will be summoned up in a language that is undeniable, and with a brightness that will, indeed, fall from the air.

(January 5, 2010)

NOTES

p. 11   **Discovery:**   This poem is based on an actual discovery by English photo-journalist Isabel Ellsen of the remains of thousands of Armenians slaughtered in a little killing field in the hill of Margada above the Syrian desert. Bestselling author and journalist Robert Fisk independently investigated and corroborated her discovery, although the car keys mentioned in my poem were used by Boghos Dakassian in digging up skulls and other bones.

p. 13   **Ceremony to Protect Mother And Child:**   A *tonir* is a clay oven (often built into the floor).

p. 14   **My Father:**   My father was about five years, four months old at the time of the Armenian genocide.

p. 19   **July in Diyarbekir:**   I am indebted to Peter Balakian for the image of partridges caught in wires.

p. 22   **Thirst:**   My father settled in Bombay during World War II, where he eventually became Works Manager of French Motors, a corporation owned and headed by Englishmen.

p. 25   **The Blindness of Infected Water:**   There was an Armenian home for the blind in Beirut. Many of the victims were young boys at the time of the genocide who had contracted a deadly virus that attacked their eyesight.

p. 26   **Dikranagerd:**   I owe my inspiration for "Dikranagerd" to Linda Pastan's "Grudnow".

p. 30   **Items Retrieved From My Father's Room:**   *The Last Days of Musa Dagh*, Franz Werfel's bestselling novel published in Germany in 1932, tells of the heroic resistance by Armenians against the Turks who invaded their mountain town in 1915. Werfel (1890-1945) was forced to flee for his life in 1938, three years after the Nazis agreed to Turkish demands to ban the book.

p. 36   **Fibonacci Poems and Variations:**   The first three poems in this sequence have a pattern of 1, 1, 2, 3, 5, and 8 syllables. The remaining ones are patterned with 1, 1, 2, 3, 5, 8 words on successive lines.

p. 38 **Eating Shoes: The Journey:** *Lavash* is soft, thin flat bread baked in a clay oven.

p. 41 **Two Photographs:** *Pasha*, a title illegal in Turkey since 1934, was used to denote men of high rank or office. It was also a title for a military commander or provincial governor in Turkey.

p. 43 **Tattooed Girls, Part One:** During the years of the slaughter, young Armenian girls were marked with specific tattoos and forced to accept Islam in exchange for their lives.

p. 48 **Thirteen Ways of Looking at 1915:** A *hammam* (from the Arabic) is a Turkish steam bath.

p. 53 **The Angels of Arshile Gorky:** Arshile Gorky's birthplace was Khorkhom. *Khor* means "deep" and *koum* "stable" in Armenian.

p. 55 **Gorky's True Name:** After watching his mother die of starvation and his family scatter in flight from the Turks, Arshile Gorky suffered a series of other catastrophes in America that deepened his acute bouts of depression and despair and that led to his suicide by hanging in 1948.

p. 56 **Gorky in Photos and Drawings:** The bastinado was a form of punishment that consisted of beating the bare soles of a person's feet with a heavy stick till they burst open.

p. 59 **Gorky's Mother:** *Tufa* is a porous rock formed as a deposit from springs or streams.

p. 61 ***Nighttime, Enigma, and Nostalgia:*** This is the title of a series of pen and ink drawings by Arshile Gorky. Khorkhom was not only Gorky's birthplace, but also another site of the mass killings.

p. 62 ***Nighttime, Enigma, and Nostalgia:*** "The melancholy of nostalgia even in peeled bodies" is a reference to Gorky's *Écorché* (c. 1931).

p. 64   ***Nighttime, Enigma, and Nostalgia:***   "Wounded birds, poverty, and one whole week of rain" and "where once the great centuries danced" are quotations from Arshile Gorky.

p. 65   **Elegy for William Saroyan:**   A famous play by Saroyan was entitled *The Time Of Your Life*. Bitlis, a town in eastern Turkey, was the birthplace of William Saroyan's ancestors.

p. 67   **Paradjanov:**   Sergei Paradjanov (1924-1990) was a Soviet Armenian painter and filmmaker who was sentenced to five years of imprisonment for homosexuality and defying the dictates of Soviet social realism. The quotation is from Paradjanov's film *Ashik Kerib* (1988).

p. 67   **Paradjanov:**   *Shadows of Forgotten Ancestors* was one of Paradjanov's most praised films. Saint Nino was the founder of Christianity in Paradjanov's birthplace.

p. 70   **Thoughts on Paradjanov's *The Colour of Pomegranates:***   Paradjanov's 1968 film is a lyrical, poetic "moving canvas" about the life of Sayat Nova, an Armenian troubadour. Abstruse and fragmented, it unfolds as tableaux with beautifully constructed images.

p. 71   **On Seeing Egoyan's *Calendar:***   Italicized quotations are from *Calendar* (1993), a film by Atom Egoyan (b. 1960), an Armenian Canadian filmmaker of international renown.

p. 73   **After Viewing *Ararat:***   Atom Egoyan's provocative film questions the nature and reliability of narrative in relation to the Armenian genocide.

p. 84   **What Follows Words:**   The quoted phrase from George Steiner's *After Babel* (Oxford, 1977, p. 183) is used in conjunction with Friedrich Holderlin (1770-1843), an important German lyric poet who had a great influence on Paul Celan (1920-1970). Celan, one of the major poets of the post-World War II era, never recovered from torture by the Nazis, and committed suicide by drowning himself in the Seine.

Adana was the centre of the last Armenian state, where genocidal events exploded in 1909.

p. 89 **Where are the Armenians in Istanbul:** *Hüzün* is a persistent melancholy. The Sufis of old defined it as the sorrow caused by the soul's separation from God.

p. 91 **The Murder of Hrant Dink:** Hrant Dink (1954-2007) was a Turkish-Armenian editor, journalist, and columnist who was prosecuted three times for "denigrating Turkishness." He received numerous death threats from Turkish nationalists, and was assassinated in Istanbul on January 9, 2007 by a young fanatic who proudly waved a Turkish flag as he was flanked by smiling policemen.

p.92 **I Who Have Not Ascended Ararat:** Raphael Patkanian's "The Tears of Araxes" is a sentimental 19th century poem in quatrains. The poet speaks to the Araxes River (that flows from the Ararat Plateau), asking why it is sad and not refreshed by nature. The river replies with an allegory about the political oppression and colonialism that have overtaken Armenia.

Abdul Hamid II (1842-1918). Paranoid and always insecure about his own safety, he turned his palace into a self-contained, garrisoned world. Despite having an Armenian mother, he decided to eliminate the Armenians by government-sanctioned mass murder.

Taner Akcam (b. October 23, 1953). Turkish historian, sociologist, and friend of the late Hrant Dink. Akcam has been denounced by Turkish authorities for his scholarly books on Turkey's culpability for the events of 1915.

KEITH GAREBIAN is a widely published, award-winning freelance literary and theatre critic, biographer, and poet. Among his many awards are the Canadian Authors Association (Niagara Branch) Poetry Award (2009), the Mississauga Arts Award (2000 and 2008), a Dan Sullivan Memorial Poetry Award (2006), and the Lakeshore Arts & Scarborough Arts Council Award for Poetry (2003). This is his fourth book of poetry.